A ROOKIE READER®

WHERE IS MITTENS?

By Kelly Boivin

Illustrations by Clovis Martin

Prepared under the direction of Robert Hillerich, Ph.D.

CHILDRENS PRESS®
CHICAGO

LIBRARY OF CONGRESS
Library of Congress Cataloging-in-Publication Data

Boivin, Kelly.
  Where is Mittens? / by Kelly Boivin ; illustrated by
Clovis Martin.
      p.   cm. — (A Rookie reader)
  Summary: A child's lost cat turns up accompanied by
four new kittens.
  ISBN 0-516-02060-9
  I. Martin, Clovis, ill. II. Title. III. Series.
  [DNLM: 1. Cats—Fiction. 2. Lost and found
possessions—Fiction.]
PZ7.B635845Wh   1990
[E]—dc20   90-2220
                                                   CIP
                                                    AC

Where is Mittens?
Where can she be?

When I called, she
didn't come to me.

"Mom, where is Mittens?
I can't find her!"

"She'll turn up, dear, never mind her."

She never goes far;
she must be near.

In her basket?

No, not here.

9

Behind the chair?

No, not there.

Under the sofa?

No, not so.

Behind the curtains?

"Dad, Mittens is gone! I really miss her!"

"Is she under the bed?"

Not a whisker!

Having a scrub?

No, she's not in the tub.

I've looked in the kitchen.

I've looked EVERYWHERE,
and I still can't find Mittens!

Hmmm . . . let me think . . .
in my closet, maybe?

YES! AND LOOK!

FOUR NEW BABIES!

"So that's why you
were hiding, Mittens!

You found a place to
have your kittens!"

WORD LIST

a	found	me	still
and	four	mind	that's
babies	goes	miss	the
basket	gone	mittens	there
be	have	Mom	think
bed	having	must	to
behind	her	my	tub
called	here	near	turn
can	hiding	never	under
can't	hmmm	new	up
chair	I	no	were
closet	in	not	when
come	is	place	where
curtains	I've	really	whisker
Dad	kitchen	scrub	why
dear	kittens	she	yes
didn't	let	she'll	you
everywhere	look	she's	your
far	looked	so	
find	maybe	sofa	

About the Author

Kelly Boivin lives in Maine with her husband, two children, two enormous dogs, and a tiger cat. They all live in semi-chaos in a hundred year old house, where things fall apart a lot more often then they get put together.

Kelly spends her days playing with blocks and finger paint as a Head Start preschool teacher, and she enjoys it very much, because she gets a lot of hugs and kisses and all the graham crackers she can eat.

She enjoys reading, cross-country skiing, camping at the beach, and, of course, writing.

This is her first published book.

About the Artist

Clovis Martin is a graduate of the Cleveland Institute of Art. During a varied career he has art directed, designed and illustrated a variety of reading, educational, and other products for children. He resides with his wife and three children in Cleveland Heights, Ohio.